KT-459-017

OF EMPIRE

ROME'S SCOTTISH FRONTIER

THE ANTONINE WALL

DAVID J. BREEZE

Principal photography by

DAVID HENRIE

Royal Commission on the Ancient and Historical Monuments of Scotland

University of Glasgow | Hunterian Museum & Art Gallery

National Museums of Scotland

BIRLINN

First published in 2008 by
Birlinn Limited
West Newington House
10 Newington Road
Edinburgh
EH9 1QS

www.birlinn.co.uk

Copyright © David Breeze 2008

The moral right of David Breeze to be identified as the author
of this work has been asserted by him in accordance with the
Copyright, Designs and Patents Act 1988.

All rights reserved. No part of this publication may be
reproduced, stored or transmitted in any form without the
express written permission of the publisher.

ISBN 13: 978 1 84158 737 0
ISBN 10: 1 84158 737 0

British Library Cataloguing-in-Publication Data
A catalogue record for this book is available from
the British Library

Designed by James Hutcheson
Typeset in MVB Verdigris
Printed and bound in Poland

WEST
DUNBARTONSHIRE
LIBRARIES

PRICE	SUPPLIER
Doo	
LOCATION	CLASS
AL	936.13
INVOICE DATE	
ACCESSION NUMBER	
C0202D 2441	

For VALERIE MAXFIELD

CONTENTS

CONTENTS

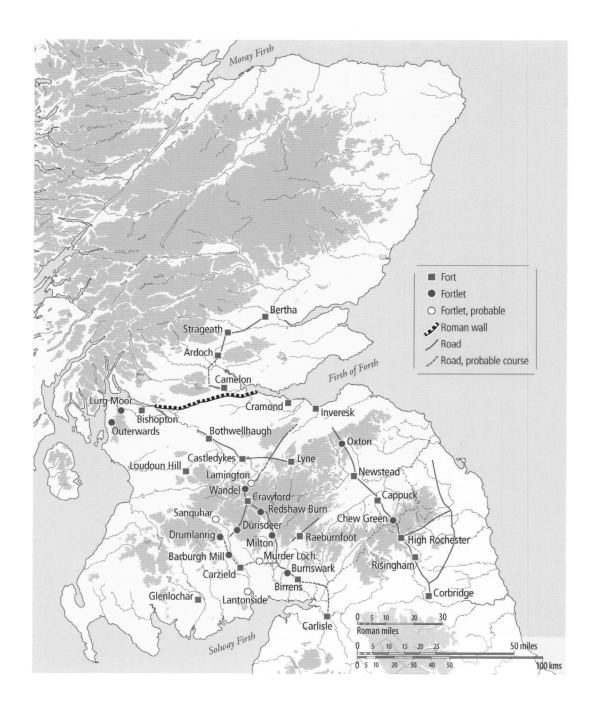

Moray Firth

Bertha

Strageath

Ardoch

Camelon

Firth of Forth

Lurg Moor
Bishopton
Outerwards

Cramond

Inveresk

Bothwellhaugh

Oxton

Castledykes

Lyne

Loudoun Hill

Lamington

Newstead

Wandel

Crawford

Cappuck

Redshaw Burn

Sanquhar

Durisdeer

Chew Green

Drumlanrig

Milton

Raeburnfoot

High Rochester

Barburgh Mill

Murder Loch

Burnswark

Risingham

Carzield

Birrens

Glenlochar

Lantonside

Corbridge

Carlisle

Solway Firth

	Fort
	Fortlet
	Fortlet, probable
	Roman wall
	Road
	Road, probable course

0 5 10 20 30
Roman miles

0 5 10 15 20 25 50 miles

0 5 10 20 30 40 50 100 kms

Roman Scotland at the time of the Antonine Wall

In the second century AD, nearly 2,000 years ago, southern Scotland was for a relatively short time brought by military force into a vast empire with Rome as its capital, though the north of the country was able to retain its freedom from conquest. Today, of our own free will, we in Scotland participate in the European Union, whose founding treaty was signed in the same city. The Antonine Wall is the most important reminder of the earlier association. It can still be traced across central Scotland. Its name survives in street signs. The artefacts from the frontier adorn our museums.

It is appropriate that this significant link with our past should have been proposed as a World Heritage Site. If successful, it will join other frontiers of the Roman empire in a great new World Heritage Site, Frontiers of the Roman Empire, and be a vital and living element in Scotland's modern international connections.

These connections are being strengthened by two international projects, the twinning of schools and museums along the frontiers of the Roman empire. Both projects will be of particular value in helping our children appreciate the international dimensions of citizenship in the twenty-first century. I wish both ventures well.

Finally, Scotland is a partner in the European Union's Culture 2000 Frontiers of the Roman Empire project. This is of particular value in informing a wider public about the Antonine Wall as well as helping archaeologists to learn more about the frontier. I am delighted that we are participating in this international project.

This one monument, the Antonine Wall, has many facets of value in today's world, from its recreational use to its international connections. For me, it is also an important example of the ability of central and local government bodies to work together for the better protection, presentation and interpretation of Scotland's premier Roman site. It is upon such co-operation that our future depends.

FOREWORD BY
Signor Gabriele Papadia de Bottini, *Italian Consul General in Scotland*

It is not by chance that the Antonine Wall is situated in a position which even at present displays interesting strategic features. The area which divides the Firth of Forth from the Firth of Clyde – in many aspects the economic heart of Scotland – is of key importance today not so much as a border, but rather as a strong road and communication link, both at intercity and international level.

Yet, thanks also to the many studies, new theories and discoveries by academics, the concept of the Roman *Limes* has acquired a rather dynamic dimension and new features are being associated with it: a frontier that can be considered not exclusively a defensive or offensive installation, but also a macro area, where Rome and its culture, even in times of conflict, found a space within the local framework.

This work by Professor David Breeze describes, in a clear and elegant manner, the profound aspects of the Roman *Limes* in Scotland and portrays an ideal guide for those who wish to recognise and appreciate an historical Scottish Italian link.

The text of a dedication to the god Mercury, erected by Italians in the Sixth Legion at Castlecary

THE NORTHERN FRONTIER

In some ways, the Roman world was not so different from our own. While there was a common thread to Rome's foreign policy over several centuries, on a shorter time-scale individual actions might move one way or the other. On succeeding his relative Trajan in 117, the new emperor, Hadrian, abandoned many of the recent conquests of his predecessor: he concentrated on strengthening the frontiers of the empire. Following Hadrian's death in 138, his successor, Antoninus Pius, abandoned the recently completed Hadrian's Wall and ordered the construction of a new frontier 120 km (75 miles) to the north, the Antonine Wall. This in turn had but a short life, of only one generation, before being abandoned after about twenty years in favour of a return to Hadrian's Wall.

The Romans were also concerned about protecting their territory, their space. As a result, their empire became surrounded and defended by a complex series of frontier installations. As a contemporary of Antoninus Pius wrote, "an encamped army like a rampart encloses the civilised world in a ring". Another said, "they surround the empire with a circle of great camps and guard so great an area of land and sea like an estate". The Antonine Wall was one such frontier. Sixty kilometres (37 miles) long, it crossed Scotland from the Firth of Forth to the River Clyde, but this linear barrier was regularly punctuated by gates. Here the regulations which governed entry into the empire would have been enforced and, presumably, customs dues collected. These were Roman Checkpoint Charlies.

If one purpose of the Antonine Wall was frontier control, another was military defence for it served as the base for a significant proportion of the army of the province. These troops were certainly necessary for the defence of the Roman province of Britain. Our literary sources record warfare on the northern frontier at various times during the second century and there may have been other events not recorded for posterity. Hadrian's reign opened with trouble in the province and forty years later the scale of the losses in Britain during his reign was still remembered. In 161 war was threatening in Britain; in about 180 "the tribes crossed the wall doing much damage and killed a general and his troops"; in 197 the situation was so serious that peace had to be bought with "a considerable sum of money", the governor recovering some of his soldiers from the enemy; in 208 the emperor himself arrived to lead a campaign against the Caledonians and their allies: two seasons of fighting followed. In these circumstances it is not surprising that there were so many forts along the Antonine Wall.

In the Roman world, as in ours, military defence never stood still but continued to develop. The Antonine Wall incorporated all the latest ideas of frontier defence. Comparison with Hadrian's Wall shows significant developments from that frontier built only a generation before. The forts were closer together and were linked by a road, beacon-platforms were provided and small enclosures constructed, all creating a closer density of military installations than before. As a single entity, the Antonine Wall can claim to have been the most complex frontier erected by the Romans.

The Antonine Wall survives remarkably well considering that it was abandoned over 1,800 years ago. Long stretches of rampart and ditch can be seen, two sections of the Military Way with, in one location, quarry pits lying beside the road, the earthworks and buildings of forts, defensive pits, a fortlet, two bath-houses and six beacon-platforms, while several museums contain the inscriptions, sculpture and artefacts recovered from the frontier.

In 2003, Scottish Ministers announced that they intended to propose the Antonine Wall as a World Heritage Site. In January 2007, the United Kingdom submitted the nomination documents to UNESCO. The decision will be taken at the meeting of the World Heritage Committee in July 2008.

The Antonine Wall crossing Croy Hill looking east: the
Wall runs from centre bottom to top right

ANTONINUS PIUS

On 10 July 138 the Emperor Hadrian died. At his death-bed was his successor, the man known to history as Antoninus Pius. It had only been six months before that Antoninus had been chosen as the heir apparent. Hadrian was childless and had been ill for some time. His first choice of successor had fallen on the young Marcus Aurelius, almost certainly a distant relation. He, however, was too young to take up the reins of government, so a stop-gap had to be found. The first choice died before Hadrian. So the dying emperor turned to the uncle-by-marriage of Marcus, a rich and elderly senator, Antoninus Pius.

Antoninus Pius had excellent credentials. He was already fifty-one, so would not delay the succession of Marcus unduly. He was well-respected: this was reflected in his nickname, Pius, which means "dutiful", though it is not certain how he obtained it. Although he had not taken a career in the emperor's service and served the normal round as an army officer and provincial governor, he had held two senior appointments and was an experienced administrator. And, perhaps importantly in Hadrian's eyes, he was not a soldier and therefore unlikely to upset Hadrian's frontier dispositions.

In fact, Hadrian miscalculated. Antoninus Pius was to live another twenty-three years, serving as emperor longer than anyone apart from the first emperor, Augustus. His relaxed attitude to government did not prepare his successors for the whirlwinds which followed their accession. And he did overturn Hadrian's frontier arrangements in Britain by abandoning Hadrian's Wall, conquering further territory to the north and ordering the construction of a new frontier, which we name in his honour, the Antonine Wall.

Bust of the Emperor Antoninus Pius dating to about 140
Coin of the Emperor Antoninus Pius dating to 142–3

Preparations

It appears that Antoninus Pius ordered action in Britain very soon after his succession. The crucial piece of evidence is an inscription from Corbridge, just south of Hadrian's Wall and on the main road north into Scotland, Dere Street. This records rebuilding here in 139, and we presume that this was part of the preparations for the advance north.

This was a practical action. It was equally important to solicit the support of the gods. The right-hand panel on the Bridgeness distance slab, found in 1868 at the eastern end of the Antonine Wall, shows a libation being poured onto an altar while a pig, sheep and bull await sacrifice. The animals are in correct order for the ceremony and this permits further interpretation of the scene.

The ceremony is the ritual cleansing of the legion and its officers prior to battle. The person pouring the libation on behalf of the Second Legion, whose flag appears behind him, was in all probability the commanding officer. This was Aulus Claudius Charax. Charax, an historian and a native of Pergamum in the province of Asia, that is modern western Turkey, was an unlikely candidate for this post. Antoninus Pius, however, had been proconsul of Asia five years before and perhaps met Charax there and later singled him out for the honour of helping extend the empire.

The stone bears evidence that it was once painted: the letters appear to have been red. Thus the title of the legion on the flag – LEG II AUG, *legio II Augusta* – was probably picked out in colour. The Second Legion Augusta had been raised by Julius Caesar and had formed part of the force invading Britain in AD 43.

The right-hand panel of the Bridgeness distance slab

The invasion

The left-hand panel of the Bridgeness distance slab relates to the next event, the invasion of north Britain. This is recorded in the *Life of Antoninus Pius*: "the emperor conquered Britain through the governor Lollius Urbicus, and, having driven back the barbarians, built a new Wall, this time of turf".

A single scene on the Bridgeness distance slab represents this activity, a Roman cavalryman riding down a group of naked enemies. One man is fallen and sheltering under his shield with a second speared from behind, while in the foreground is a man in a pose of subjugation and another, apparently bound, beheaded. An alternative explanation is that the scene reflects a series of separate actions in relation to one man; a sort of cinematic effect.

The scene, in its general elements, is a standard format and therefore the details should perhaps not be taken literally, as, for example, an indication that the men of north Britain fought naked – rather unlikely in the northern climate!

Roman cavalry would certainly have been included in the invasion force. The core of the army was composed of soldiers of the three legions of the province, the Second, Sixth and Twentieth, based in Caerleon, York and Chester respectively. The Second Legion was present at full strength, in theory about 5,000 strong, while the other two provided detachments of unknown size. These would have been supported by regiments drawn from the other main branch of the provincial army, the *auxilia*. There were six different types of auxiliary regiments, 500 or 1,000 strong, infantry or cavalry, or mixed.

The army on the march

Trajan's Column in Rome records the warfare of an earlier generation, the conquest of Dacia, modern Romania, by the Emperor Trajan between 101 and 106. This scene on the Column depicts a Roman army on the march. The army is crossing a bridge of boats. At the head of the column of legionaries are their officers and standard bearers. These carry the eagle, the emblem of the legion, and the standards of the individual centuries. The soldiers are in armour, but march bareheaded. The ordinary soldiers wear armour formed of metal strips, and carry rectangular shields (see page 53), while the standard bearers, seen here, are in mail or scale armour and have oval shields. The officer wears a cloak, the standard bearers bear-skins.

Several Roman writers described the order of march. In 135, shortly before Lollius Urbicus began his campaign, Flavius Arrianus, governor of Cappodocia on the eastern frontier, recorded his order of march as he proceeded against the Alans. In the advance guard were the scouts, followed by the cavalry drawn from the auxiliary regiments. The infantry followed, the auxiliary units in front and then two legions with further auxiliary units behind, all flanked by cavalry. At the rear was the baggage with a cavalry regiment forming the rear guard. The strength of this force was 22,000 soldiers, split almost equally between legions and auxiliary regiments and perhaps not very different in size from the force which Lollius Urbicus led. The column of marching men would have been long: Ammianus Marcellinus recorded that the Emperor Julian's column of 30,000 men in his 363 campaign stretched for 15 km (nearly 10 miles) across the landscape.

Scene on Trajan's Column showing soldiers on the march

VICTORY

The gods smiled on the Romans and they were victorious, though no doubt their use of overwhelming force and the operations of a trained, disciplined and well-armed army played a part. On the Hutcheson Hill distance slab, found in 1969, the goddess Victory is shown at the end of the campaign placing a wreath in the beak of the legion's eagle, held by the standard bearer, the event being observed by two bound and kneeling captives.

The victory was achieved by 1 August 142, the date of the first record of Antoninus Pius being acclaimed *Imperator*, Conqueror, for the second time: his earlier acclamation had been honorary, acknowledging his adoption by Hadrian. Bearing in mind that it will have taken many weeks for news to travel from Britain to Rome, it is possible that the fighting had ended in the previous season. A coin issue in 142 or early the next year celebrated the victory. An account of a speech, probably made in the Senate in Rome in 142, also refers to the same event. The speaker was Cornelius Fronto, tutor to the prince Marcus Aurelius, a member of the imperial court and, in this year, consul. "Although he [that is, Antoninus] had committed the conduct of the campaign to others while sitting at home himself in the Palace at Rome, yet like the helmsman at the tiller of a ship of war, the glory of the whole navigation and voyage belonged to him." Hyperbole certainly, but it does remind us that decisions relating to the extension of the empire were taken by the emperor himself.

The victory, therefore, was celebrated on coins and inscriptions across the empire, and, significantly, in spite of other wars during his long reign, Antoninus Pius was not again to take the title *Imperator*. The overwhelming impression is that this event was of special significance for the new emperor.

The purpose of the distance slabs

The stone shown opposite stood at the west end of the Antonine Wall. The goddess Victory is shown sitting in front of her temple. The pediment is supported by fluted columns with Corinthian capitals. The goddess holds a palm leaf in one hand and a laurel wreath in the other, while one arm rests on a globe.

The distance slabs of the Antonine Wall are very ornate for military sculpture on Roman frontiers. Such sculptural records are not found on Hadrian's Wall, where the building records were very simple, nor on the German frontier constructed later in the reign of Antoninus Pius. Furthermore, the sculpture is unusual for any frontier, perhaps only bearing comparison with the great military monument at Adamklissi in Romania.

The reason for the decoration of the Antonine Wall with this ornate sculpture may be found in the nature of succession of Antoninus Pius. It would have been known in Rome that he was not Hadrian's first choice as successor. In these circumstances, it would be understandable if Antoninus Pius wished to stamp his own authority on his succession by obtaining a military victory and recording it so spectacularly. Perhaps, therefore, the main purpose of the distance slabs was to glorify the conquests of the new emperor and testify to the support which the gods gave to him in achieving this success.

Distance slabs were erected on both the north as well as the south faces of the Antonine Wall. A cramp hole on the back of this stone, and similar devices on others, offers a hint that they were attached to structures of some kind.

This distance slab stood at Ferrydyke at the west end of the Antonine Wall. It was acquired by Glasgow University from the Marquis of Montrose at the end of the seventeenth century.

The location of the Antonine Wall

Central Scotland offered a superb location for the Antonine Wall. Here is the Midland Valley, a rift valley between two fault lines. This valley is now occupied to the east by the River Carron, a tributary of the Forth, and to the west by the River Kelvin, a tributary of the Clyde. The Antonine Wall was placed upon the south side of the valley, overlooking the rivers to the north. The valley is so flat in places that it readily floods even today, and before drainage in the eighteenth century must have been much boggier, which may account for the lack of cavalry attested on the frontier.

To the north of the Midland Valley rise the Campsie Fells, here flecked with snow. Work on past environments suggests that people used this landscape, but little

trace of this activity is visible today, and few remains of settlements have been found on the Fells; perhaps they were mainly used for grazing.

The rift valley, and the raised beach to the east, formed a convenient location for the Antonine Wall. To the west, however, no such topographical feature existed, and as a result, after crossing the River Kelvin at Balmuildy, the Wall jumped from one high point to another before reaching the north shore of the River Clyde, perhaps at a low enough point to guard most of the fording places.

The Kelvin Valley looking west from the Iron Age fort on Castle Hill (see page 33)

Surveying the line

While the geography of the area largely dictated the location of the Wall, the line still had to be surveyed. The Roman army included surveyors and these will have marked out the route to be taken by the frontier. Whereas Hadrian's Wall was often laid out in straight stretches, the Antonine Wall adapted itself more closely to the country, its route being more sinuous as it followed the lie of the land.

At the very centre of the frontier, the Wall climbed over two hills, Croy Hill and Bar Hill. Croy Hill and Castle Hill beside Bar Hill are formed of dolerite and in several locations the hardness of the rock defeated the soldiers digging the ditch. Otherwise, the Wall swept over the hills, relating itself to the landscape. In this view, the Wall climbs up the east slope of Croy Hill before swinging to the right on gaining the summit, all the way hugging the edge of the crags.

Interestingly, a small enclosure has been found on both Bar Hill and Croy Hill, in each case beneath the Antonine Wall fort. It has been suggested that these were in some way connected to the survey of or other preparations for the construction of the Wall in the central sector. The shallow ditch of the enclosure on the top of Bar Hill can still seen around the headquarters building (see page 58).

The landscape of Croy Hill, moorland today, bears the record of many past Roman activities. A hamlet sat within the fort, marked by the trees centre left, while heaps of waste from former mining activities lie to the right. The west side of the hill was quarried for road stone. In the distance is the village of Croy built for the workmen.

Disrupting the locals

The Antonine Wall cut right across the countryside, rather like a modern motorway. It crossed farmland, route-ways and presumably split families, who suddenly found themselves separated by the earthworks, rather like the inhabitants of Berlin in the 1960s or Israel and Palestine at the present day. While archaeological and botanical research has demonstrated that the Wall was built in a fairly open landscape, with some woodland, the predominant impression that the soldiers would have gained was of a settled farming community, tilling the land as they had done for at least 3,000 years. Unfortunately, we have found little evidence of pre-Roman farming along the Antonine Wall, unlike on Hadrian's Wall where plough marks have been found at about a dozen places on the frontier below the military installations, and there are few known traces of indigenous settlements in the immediately vicinity of the Wall.

Next to the Wall, at Bar Hill, however, sits a small hill fort, probably long abandoned when the Wall was built. Its ramparts and ditches can now be traced as a series of shelves round the northern half of the small hill on which it sits, Castle Hill visible in the centre of the photograph. The hill is formed of dolerite, a hard volcanic rock, and this defeated the Roman soldiers digging the ditch of the Antonine Wall, which is uncut to the north (left) of the hill fort. It does not seem likely, therefore, that the ditches of the pre-Roman hill fort could have been very deep. Ironically, the civil settlement outside the Roman fort on Bar Hill appears to have grown up in the shadow of its Iron Age predecessor. The south side of the hill has been quarried away in modern times.

The Wall crossing Bar Hill from bottom centre to top right, curving round Castle Hill; the trig point shown on pages 28–29 can be seen on top of the hill

IMP·C·T·AELIO·HADRI
ANO·ANTONINO·AVG
P·P·VEX·LEG·XX
V·V·F·EC·S·P·F
O·I·V·S·V·E·I·P·F
M·M·M·CCXI·I

The name of the Antonine Wall

Each distance slab records the name of Antoninus Pius, the legion and the distance erected. The distance was mostly recorded in paces, but the western 6.5 km (4 miles) were measured in feet. The sections recorded in paces were much longer than those in feet – for example, 4,652 paces (about $4^2/_3$ miles), 3,666 paces ($3^2/_3$ miles) or 3,000 paces (3 miles) compared, for instance, with 4,411, 3,271, 3,000 feet – so the use of feet gave a spurious similarity to the measurements, though the total length constructed in feet was less than the $4^2/_3$ miles built by the Second Legion at the other end of the Wall.

The distances were carefully tabulated, in two cases $3,666^1/_2$ and $3,660 \ ^4/_5$ paces. This emphasises the precision which went into the task of surveying and building the Antonine Wall. The known distances also suggest that the central sector was the first to be constructed, from modern Seabegs in Bonnybridge to Castlehill in Bearsden. One distance slab found here recorded $3,660 \ ^4/_5$ paces built by the Twentieth Legion; a second, from an unknown location, 3,000 paces. The total, $6,660 \ ^4/_5$ paces, when multiplied by three for the three legions comes to almost exactly half the length of the Wall, which cannot be a coincidence. It seems possible that the eastern 22 km (13 miles) were built next, with the western 6.5 km (3 miles) forming the last section.

The Braidfield distance slab records the name given to the operation: *opus valli*, the work of the wall. This only appears on one other stone, also erected by the Sixth Legion. Not all the distance slabs are as highly decorated as this stone. Winged Victories support the panel bearing the inscription, flanked by Mars and Valour, the latter holding a flag on which is inscribed VIRT AVG, *Virtus Augusta*, The Valour of the Emperor.

DATING THE ANTONINE WALL

The *Life of Antoninus Pius*, written about two hundred years after his death, records that the emperor won his victory in Britain through his general Lollius Urbicus. Urbicus was a native of north Africa. Interestingly, he was not the eldest son in his family, so he must have possessed considerable talent to rise so high in the emperor's service. Nor was his appointment to Britain – and the glory of obtaining a victory for his emperor – his last achievement. He ended his career as one of the top officials of the empire, Prefect of the City of Rome. In this capacity he had a seat on the emperor's inner council of advisors.

Lollius Urbicus not only achieved victory in Britain, in 141 or 142, but started the programme of building the Antonine Wall. We know this because his name is recorded on this building inscription found at Balmuildy: fragments of a second stone bearing his name were found lying on the road surface at the north gate of the fort during its excavation in 1912. The stone illustrated here was found in the seventeenth century and described by the eighteenth-century antiquary Alexander Gordon as the "most invaluable Jewel of Antiquity" for it confirmed the statement that Lollius Urbicus built the Wall.

The name of Lollius Urbicus does not appear on any other inscription on the Antonine Wall. Excavation has demonstrated that Balmuildy was one of the first forts to be built on the Wall, being laid out before the Antonine Wall rampart arrived at the site. Perhaps Urbicus supervised the surveying of the line of the frontier, and the start of building, and then relinquished his command, leaving the remainder of the work to his successor.

Building inscription at Balmuildy

IMP · C · T · AEL · HADR
ANTONINO · AVG · PIO
P · P · LEG · II · AVG · SVB
Q · LOLLIO · VRBICO
N LEG · AVG · PR · PR · FEC

F.19

Outline of camp

Outline of camp

BUILDING THE WALL

The soldiers building the Antonine Wall required accommodation. They slept in tents made of leather arranged in rows within the protection of a rampart and ditch. None of these labour camps along the Antonine Wall are visible today, but about twenty have been discovered through aerial survey, while excavations have revealed useful details about several.

The anonymous Roman writer whom we call Pseudo-Hyginus specified the appropriate dimensions for the camp defences: the ditch should be at least 5 Roman feet (1.5 m) wide and 3 feet (1 m) deep in front of a rampart 9 feet (3 m) wide and 6 feet (2 m) high. The fourth-century Roman writer Vegetius offers rather larger figures for the ditch, 9 feet (3 m) wide and 7 feet (2.3 m) deep, but less for the rampart, 3 feet (1m) high, though he noted that in a threatening situation the defences should be more substantial. For this work, he stated, soldiers should carry mattocks, rakes, baskets and other types of tools. Pseudo-Hyginus recorded that each entrance should be protected by a detached length of ditch.

Most of the camps along the Antonine Wall are about the same size, 2 ha (nearly 5 acres) or a little larger. At the east end of the Wall, four camps have been found from the air in the 4²/₃-mile sector built by the Second Legion. Two lie at each end of this sector, and two more camps lie at the east end of the next sector to the west. This suggests that the soldiers of these two legions worked from each end towards the middle. Camps also provide a hint at the complexity of the building programme, with, for example, two phases of use in the camp at Dullatur.

The labour camp at Tamfourhill. The ditch of the camp is identifiable as a darker line in the field, with an entrance visible to each side.

THE ANTONINE WALL | 39

The rampart

Hadrian's Wall, for reasons we do not understand, was built partly of stone and partly of turf. The Antonine Wall was constructed of earth. Mostly turfs were used, but in the eastern sector clay was the main material of construction, while sometimes earth was piled between cheeks of turf. In all cases, the turf, earth or clay was placed on a stone base.

Although the *Life of Antoninus Pius* stated that the Wall built by Lollius Urbicus was constructed of turf, this was not conclusively demonstrated until the excavations of the Glasgow Archaeological Society in the 1890s. A section drawn at this time reveals a 30 degree slope to the rear face of the rampart.

It is not known how high this rampart would have stood. The 1890s', excavators recorded nineteen layers of turf-work and Kenneth Steer as many as twenty at Bonnyside in 1957. Vegetius stated that each turf should measure 18 by 12 by 6 Roman inches thick (450 by 300 by 150 mm). On that basis, the rampart may have stood about 10 Roman feet (3 m) high. It is not known how the top was completed. The contemporary frontier in Germany was a stout fence, with no rampart walk, so we do not necessarily have to presume that a breastwork and walkway surmounted the Antonine Wall. The purpose of the Wall was perhaps to serve more as a demarcation line rather than as a military defensive line. Indeed, the Roman army was not equipped to fight defensively from ramparts and fort walls, preferring to operate in the field where its discipline, training and weapons gave it a significant advantage.

The rampart and ditch at Rough Castle looking east

THE STONE BASE

It would appear that the stone base of the Antonine Wall was intended to be 15 Roman feet (4.44 m) wide, though its width does vary. The kerbs of the stone base were dressed, but the mass of stones in between them were rough cobbles or blocks of various sizes. The purpose of the stone base would have been to aid stability. It also helped water to drain from the base of the rampart. In order to aid drainage and prevent ponding on one side of the Wall, culverts were provided within the base. This stone base was an improvement on the turf section of Hadrian's Wall, which had simply been placed upon a turf base.

At some places evidence appears to exist for the points at which the different gangs working on the base met. In New Kilpatrick Cemetery, two such possible junctions may be noted, one in each section. In one length, there are several stones in a line across part of the base. In the other section, the distinction is emphasised by the different size of stones used in the base.

The stone base and the rampart above it, together with all the structures along the Wall, would have been planned by the architect-engineers who served in the legions. One such soldier is recorded at Birrens in modern Dumfriesshire; his inscription is now in the National Museum of Scotland.

THE DITCH

The rampart was fronted by a wide and deep ditch. This is best preserved at Watling Lodge in Falkirk. Here is it 12 m (40 ft) wide and 4 m (12 ft) deep, probably close to its original size. The sides were cut to angles of 30 degrees. This was a substantial obstacle. But the ditch was only excavated to such a size for about a quarter of its total length of 60 km (37 miles). These 16 km (10 miles) run from Watling Lodge westwards through the most spectacular surviving length of the frontier to the highest point of the Wall on Bar Hill. Study of the distance slabs suggests that this was part of the earliest constructed sector of the Wall. To the east of Watling Lodge the width varies from 6.1 m to 10.7 m (20 to 35 ft), while to the west of Bar Hill the ditch rarely exceeded 7.6 m (25 ft) in width. These variations may reflect the actions of different legions, though we do not know enough to be able to prove this.

The material extracted from the ditch was tipped out onto the north side to form a wide, low bank, the outer or upcast mound, a glacis in military terminology, generally much wider than the ditch. Some excavations have revealed that the turf was not removed before the earth was dumped on top. This suggests that there was plentiful pasture in the vicinity of the Wall to provide the great quantities of turf needed in the construction of the rampart. Pollen analysis has been able to corroborate this. The woodland canopy had therefore largely been removed before the Roman army arrived in northern Britain.

The ditch at Watling Lodge

The ditch on Croy Hill

Even on Croy Hill and Bar Hill, where the land sloped steeply to the north, a ditch was provided. It was still substantial on the east slope of Croy Hill, attaining the width of that at Watling Lodge, 12 m (40 ft), though the hard dolerite rock precluded cutting of the ditch to the same depth. It is only about 2.4 m (8 ft) deep, with substantial boulders still obtruding from the sides of the ditch.

Just to the east of the fort, for a distance of 24 m (80 ft), the ditch is unfinished. One early visitor, William Maitland, who visited the spot in the eighteenth century, could not believe that the Roman soldiers had failed to complete their task and to explain the mystery he offered the theory that rock vegetates or grows.

In the photograph, this stretch of uncut ditch may be seen in the foreground. Beyond, the ditch is shallow, being mostly filled with silt. To the left, the trees sit on the site of the fort at Croy Hill; the site of the next fort at Bar Hill is visible in the far distance to the right. In the middle distance, the rampart passes over the top of the hill and, as the slope steepens, the ditch moves away and drops lower down the crags to the right, in deep shadow on this photograph. Its width decreases, sometimes to as little as 6 m (20 ft), but, with only the occasional exception, it was still completed, "hewn out with unrelenting persistence", as Sir George Macdonald eloquently recorded in the early twentieth century.

THE MILITARY WAY

The final linear element was a road, the Military Way. Enough of this has been found to suggest that originally it ran along the whole length of the Wall, normally between 36 and 46 m (120 to 150 ft) south of the rampart. The road was formed of stones with a surface of gravel: at Rough Castle excavation revealed that the stones were placed on a bed of turf. The resulting all-weather surface was about 5 m (16 ft) wide, with side ditches helping drainage.

Two writers provide useful information about the Roman army on the march. The Jewish writer Josephus, writing in the late first century AD, stated that the Roman infantry marched six abreast. Flavius Arrianus writing just a few years before the construction of the Antonine Wall, however, recorded that his legion marched four abreast. Both were military men – Josephus was an officer in the Jewish army while Arrianus was governor of Cappadocia under Hadrian – and both must have been writing from personal knowledge. Perhaps the difference reflected the local conditions. Certainly, the width of the Military Way would not allow soldiers to march six abreast.

The Military Way appears to have been planned from the beginning, because at Rough Castle a quarry pit, dug to obtain stone for use in the road, was found below a primary feature of the frontier, an 'expansion'/beacon-platform. The purpose of the road was to aid communication, in particular between the forts.

The Military Way probably survives well in Seabegs Wood because this ancient wood has protected the archaeological remains. We know that Seabegs Wood was already defined within its present boundaries in 1787, and it remains an important natural resource in central Scotland.

Rough Castle fort

The fort known as Rough Castle survives today as a series of earthworks, the best on the line of the Antonine Wall. It was first described over three hundred years ago. "About two miles [3.2 km] from the Maiden Castle is a large square work of stone with a double ditch about it. The common people hereabouts call it *Castle Ruff.* Here are the ruins of several stone buildings. About the middle of the square is an overture thro which shepherd boys creep into a Vault underneath." This 'vault' may be the hypocaust of the bath-house or the stone-lined tank found beside the headquarters building in 1961.

The fort was planned by John Horsley in 1732 and again by William Roy in 1755. The site was chosen by the Society of Antiquaries of Scotland to be the subject of their excavation in 1902–3, and it was examined again in 1920, 1932–3 and 1957–61. These investigations have revealed three stone buildings – a central headquarters building, (*principia* in Latin) a house for the commanding officer and a granary – and timber buildings, presumably barrack-blocks. The annexe contained a stone bath-house.

The fort is almost square, surrounded by two ditches. To the east (right) is an annexe, with one ditch to the south and, inexplicably, three to the east. The Military Way passes through the centre of the fort and the annexe, though here its width is increased from 5.5 m to about 12 m (18 to 40 ft). To its north, and immediately outside the east gate of the fort but obscured by trees, is a small enclosure. Interpreted as a wagon-park by the early excavators, it may be the remains of a fortlet built before the fort. A building inscription attests that the fort was erected by soldiers of the Sixth Cohort of Nervians, which is also recorded on an altar found south of the fort in 1843.

Soldiers at work

A few years before the construction of the Antonine Wall, Trajan's Column was erected in Rome. This monument indicates how the soldiers went about the business of building forts, and although there is an element of artist's license in these depictions, the basic aspects are clear. Here, soldiers are using turf to build the rampart of a fort. The soldier beside the gate is about to be relieved of the turf block which he is carrying on his shoulders, held on by what appears to be a short length of rope. The Jewish historian Josephus, writing in the late first century, listed what every soldier should carry in addition to his armour and weapons: a saw and basket, axe and pick, strap, billhook, chain and three days' rations. The strap and the chain would both be appropriate for holding the turf block in place. The shoulders are a sensible place to carry a substantial turf block; held in the hands, it will fall and break.

In the foreground, soldiers are cutting turf blocks, while their comrades are removing earth from the ditch; it is being carried away in wicker baskets. A walkway of logs along the top of the fort rampart has been laid down and a breastwork erected.

The soldiers are working in armour, and the armour indicates that they were legionaries. To one side, their spears, shields and helmets have been placed ready for immediate uplift should they be attacked.

Scene on Trajan's Column showing soldiers building a fort

THE *LILIA*

The early twentieth-century excavators made a remarkable discovery at Rough Castle. Cutting a section across the northern defences, they uncovered a series of pits north of the upcast mound. These lay in ten rows, in the words of the excavators "arranged obliquely, so that pit and level surface alternate either way". The pits protect a length of 60 m (200 ft) across the north side of the fort from the north gate to the edge of the bank of the little valley in which sits the Rowan Tree Burn.

Each pit measures 2.1 m by 0.9 m and is 760 mm deep (6 by 3 by 2 ft 6 in): from centre to centre they are 3 m (10 ft) one way and 1.5 m (5 ft) the other. No artefacts were found in any pit.

The pits were soon likened to the description Julius Caesar provided of obstacles he had ordered to be dug when besieging the town of Alesia in Gaul in 52 BC. There he dug eight rows of pits in a diagonal formation. They were 1 m (3 ft) apart and the same depth, tapering towards the bottom. In each was placed a sharpened stake firmly embedded in the ground with the remainder of the space filled with twigs and brushwood to hide the trap. Caesar's soldiers called them *lilia* after the flower.

Over the last two decades similar arrangements of pits have been found on the berm – the space between the rampart and the ditch – in various locations on both the Antonine Wall and Hadrian's Wall. They are usually arranged in a quincunx – that is diagonal – formation. At Byker in Newcastle on Hadrian's Wall the impressions of two stakes were found in each pit.

The west defences of Rough Castle

The fort at Rough Castle sits on the right bank of the Rowan Tree Burn. While its northern approach was protected by the *lilia*, rather surprisingly, an extra ditch was provided on its western flank between the stream and the two main fort ditches. This seems superfluous, but it is interesting that the defences of several forts on the Antonine Wall were stronger than the minimum normal requirement. This is particularly noteworthy at Rough Castle, whose north approach was protected by the *lilia* while the annexe was protected by three ditches to the east.

Rough Castle fort is not unusual in the irregular provision of ditches. Few forts on the Antonine Wall had the same number of ditches round the whole circuit of the defences. Most had two ditches, with three on at least one side: Mumrills had four to the west. At Bearsden, there was only one ditch to the south of the fort, but it was twice the size of a normal ditch.

In this view, the ditch of the Antonine Wall is in shadow, with the upcast mound to its left and the platform of the fort to its right.

The west defences of the fort at Rough Castle and the plan prepared in 1904

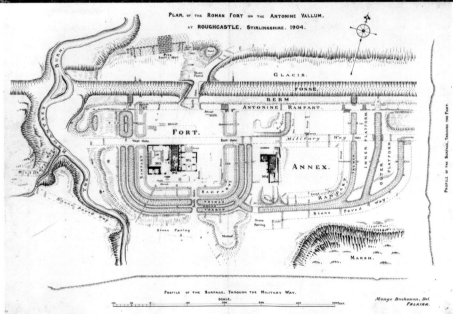

PLAN. OF THE ROMAN FORT ON THE ANTONINE VALLUM.
AT ROUGHCASTLE. STIRLINGSHIRE. 1904.

Bar Hill fort

The highest fort on the Antonine Wall was on Bar Hill. This was not attached to the Antonine Wall rampart but was placed a little to the south on the highest point of the hill. The platform of the fort is visible; within the defences two buildings have been excavated and laid out. One is the headquarters building placed in the centre of the fort. The building contained a courtyard, where notices were probably displayed, an assembly hall and rooms for the regimental clerks. Here the clerks maintained the regimental records including the soldiers' personal files, pay records, duty rosters, applications for leave and the annual returns to Rome. The other building was the bath-house, tucked into the north-west corner of the fort, bottom left.

The fort was examined in 1902–5 when several buildings were excavated, including the timber barrack-blocks, and again in 1978–82. The well, now visible in the courtyard of the headquarters building, was found on the first morning of the excavation. It yielded a rich harvest of finds, including columns, capitals and other building stones, wooden beams, an altar, a dedication slab, ballista balls, coins, arrowheads, pottery, tools, animal bones and shells, and part of the frame, pulley and bucket. Many of these finds are now on display in the Hunterian Museum of the University of Glasgow.

Two regiments are known to have been stationed at this fort, though presumably not at the same time. These were the First Cohort of Baetasians, originally raised from the Lower Rhineland, and the First Cohort of Hamians from Syria. The appearance of the Baetasians on a dedication slab suggests that they may have built or repaired the fort: the unit is also attested at Old Kilpatrick at the very west end of the Wall. Further inscriptions record work by the Second and Twentieth Legions at Bar Hill.

An artist's impression of Bar Hill fort

This artist's impression of the fort on Bar Hill by Michael J. Moore shows the fort from the south-east. The headquarters building sits in the centre of the fort, its assembly hall standing above the rest of the building. To its right is a large granary, beside which two smaller buildings have been restored in this drawing. The house of the commanding officer has been placed to the left of the headquarters building, though in many forts it lies to the right. To north and south are barrack-blocks and in the top corner of the fort is the bath-house. The scale of the accommodation depended on rank. The commanding officer had his own house in which also lived his wife and children – women's and children's shoes have been found at Bar Hill – and his slaves, while up to eight soldiers shared one barrack-room.

There was no special provision for the soldiers to eat together. Each soldier was issued with his own food and cooked it himself, though in reality several soldiers probably banded together in mess groups. In the summer, meals may have been eaten outdoors, in the winter presumably in the barrack-room.

The bath-house and the buildings in the central range were built of stone, and possibly had tile roofs. The barrack-blocks were of timber, possibly with thatch roofs. The walls of the barrack-blocks were formed of timber uprights, with wattles woven in between and the whole coated with daub: plaster was then possibly applied. Some window glass has been found in the fort, and also possible metal frames to hold glass panes.

Some discoveries suggest that a civil settlement may have lain beyond the fort outside the east gate, perhaps straddling the Military Way.

An artist's impression of Bar Hill fort by Michael J. Moore

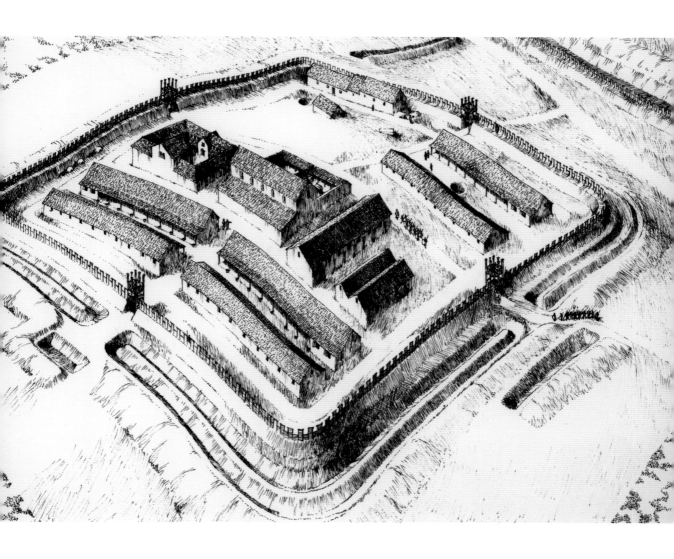

The bath-house at Bar Hill

The forts on the Antonine Wall are somewhat unusual in Britain in that several contain a regimental bath-house: normally this building was placed outside the fort. It is usually suggested that this was because of the risk of fire within the fort, but this seems unlikely as many forts contained ovens and other cooking areas and possibly also hearths where fires could be lit to heat barrack-rooms.

The bath-house at Bar Hill is tucked into the lee of the north rampart of the fort to the west of the north gate. Its rooms were arranged in a long line. At the west end was a changing room containing a latrine. The next room was the cold room. Unusually, neither room possessed a north wall so presumably this was formed by the inside face of the rampart; a similar arrangement existed in the latrine at Bearsden.

There were three heated rooms, with the furnace at the east end, part of which is seen in this photograph. At one point during the life of the fort, a small pottery kiln was constructed here. Its use would have prevented access to the furnace. Pottery in an African style was made in the kiln. It is possible that soldiers were sent from Britain to serve in the Moorish War of Antoninus Pius and, if so, their return in about 150 could account for the African influence.

The bath-house was modified during its life, with a second furnace added within the building. Part of the raised floor and supporting pillars of the room heated by this furnace can be seen in this photograph.

The bath-house at Bar Hill looking west

KINNEIL FORTLET

The fortlet at Kinneil was discovered as a result of field walking in 1976; later the whole site was excavated under the aegis of Falkirk Council and laid out for public inspection. The outline of the enclosure can be seen, two gates, and modern posts replicating internal timber buildings. The surrounding ditch and interior well were back-filled at the end of the excavation.

Kinneil is one of at least nine fortlets discovered along the line of the Antonine Wall, while enough evidence survives to suggest the former existence of another five. They measure about 21 m by 18 m (70 ft by 60 ft) internally. The purpose of the fortlet was presumably to allow for movement through the frontier. Here, we may suppose, were enforced the regulations which we know were applied in Germany to govern entry into the empire. Travellers were only allowed to pass through specified points, and to travel unarmed to named meeting places or markets, usually under military escort. At such frontier points, customs dues were also possibly collected.

There is, however, an anomaly on the Antonine Wall. Although fortlets and forts had north gates, in several cases no causeway exists over the ditch beyond. Were causeways once provided only to be later removed? Excavation may be able to provide an answer. Examination of the north gate of the fortlet at Kinneil has shown that the gate structure was dismantled at some point during the life of the enclosure and a drain cut across the site of the east gate timbers; this may relate to the removal of a causeway. Excavations have demonstrated that the nature of the occupation of other fortlets also changed, buildings being removed and part, or all, of the internal area surfaced with cobbles.

Kinneil fortlet from the air and its north gate

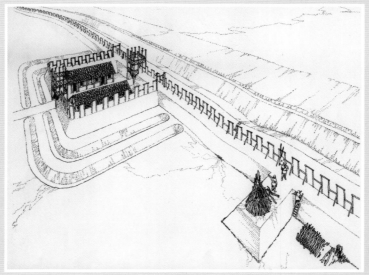

Bonnyside East 'Expansion'

Along the Antonine Wall are several unusual features. They are southern 'expansions' of the rampart, each forming a distinct mound behind the Wall: one is visible top-left on this photograph. There are six known examples of this type of structure and they are found in pairs. Two lie to the west of the fort at Rough Castle; this is Bonnyside East.

The two pairs found east and west of Rough Castle fort have wide views to the north, up the Firth of Forth towards the outpost forts. The pair on the west brow of Croy Hill have wide, all-round views to north, west and south. Perhaps the view south to the hinterland fort at Bothwellhaugh was the most significant.

Bonnyside East 'expansion' was excavated in 1957. A stone base 5.2 m (17 ft) square was placed to the rear of the Antonine Wall rampart. It was clearly built after the rampart base because some cobbles of the expansion overlapped the base. However, the turf superstructure of the base and the platform were built together as there was no clear division between the turves of the two and indeed several lines of turf carried across the two structures. A quarry pit from which stone was extracted for use in the construction of the Military Way was found below the base; it had been filled with turfs before the base was laid down.

Burnt wood and turf-work were found around the square base, as well as fragments of two Roman pottery vessels. This allowed the excavator, Kenneth Steer, to suggest that fires had been lit on top of the 'expansion' and that soldiers spent some time there on duty. The conclusion was that the 'expansions' were probably beacon-platforms for signalling.

Soldiers of the Wall

While the Antonine Wall was built by the crack troops of the Roman army, the legions, the soldiers who manned its forts and undertook the duties of frontier control were drawn from the *auxilia*. These had originally been so named because they supported the legions. These regiments were provided by the allies and friends of Rome, and later the frontier tribes. They retained their original names, such as the Fourth Cohort of Gauls, which was based at Castlehill fort. However, once settled in a new base, each regiment tended to recruit locally. Hence, a soldier, Nectovelius, a Brigantian by birth from what is now northern England, was stationed at Mumrills, where he died and where his tombstone was erected. His unit was the Second Cohort of Thracians, which had been raised in what is now Bulgaria.

Both infantry and cavalry were based on the Antonine Wall. This painting of two auxiliary soldiers by Peter Connolly includes an infantryman and, holding the horse's reins, a cavalryman, recognisable from his more elaborate helmet. Both men were clad in mail shirts and carried an oval shield, a spear and a sword, the cavalryman's being longer.

Somewhat unusually, legionaries are recorded at four forts along the line of the Wall, apparently based there as opposed to being part of the building party. This may suggest that the occupation of the Antonine Wall overstretched the manpower resources of the Roman army in Britain and led to the unusual use of legionaries as frontier troops.

A cavalryman and an infantryman (above) and legionary (below) painted by Peter Connolly

Bearsden bath-house

The forts on the Antonine Wall were provided with facilities intended to ensure the comfort and health of the soldiers. The Roman army appreciated that disease was as much a foe as any human enemy. As a result, regiments were provided with doctors, forts with hospitals, and also with flush-water latrines and bath-houses.

The bath-house at Bearsden was provided for the use of a small garrison of perhaps no more than 120 men. Yet, it contained both a steam bath and sauna. The former we refer to as a Turkish bath, because such baths were still in use in Constantinople when it was conquered by the Turks: it should be termed a Roman bath!

In this view, the corner of the timber changing room lies to the right, with the cold room to its left. This led into the three rooms and the hot bath of the steam range, or to the hot dry room to the left with its own furnace, and to the apsidal cold bath to the right. Top left is part of an earlier bath-house, demolished before completion. The water from the bath-house was led through drains to the bottom end of the site where the latrine was placed.

The bath-house at Bearsden
The head of the goddess Fortuna found in the bath-house

The Bearsden latrine

Outside the bath-house at Bearsden lay a latrine. No less than four drains led water from the bath-house to the latrine. Accordingly, this had a plentiful supply of water to flush the sewage away. The refuse from the latrine passed along a drain through the rampart and was discharged into the fort ditch. When the fort was abandoned, the east ditches were almost half full of sewage!

During the excavations of the fort in the 1970s the sewage from the latrine was found and samples taken. These provided plentiful evidence on the soldier's diet. The sewage contained fragments of wheat, barley, bean, fig, dill, coriander, opium poppy (possibly used on bread as today), hazelnut, raspberry, bramble, wild strawberry, bilberry and celery. Fig, dill, coriander and celery, the seeds of which were used as spices and also medicinally, may have been imported from the Mediterranean. Analysis of the sterols in the sewage indicated that the balance of the diet was mainly vegetarian. Indeed, no bones were found at Bearsden, but that must have been because the acidity of the soil had destroyed them. There is plentiful literary, documentary and archaeological evidence to demonstrate that Roman soldiers ate meat. Perhaps it was simply that, before the days of refrigeration, less meat was eaten over the winter owing to difficulties of preservation.

Analysis of the sewage also demonstrated that the soldiers had whipworm and roundworm, and that some of the grain was contaminated with weevils. Moss found in the sewage was probably used by the soldiers to wipe themselves, though elsewhere a sponge on a stick was used for this purpose.

Artist's impression of the latrine at Bearsden by Michael J. Moore

Supplying the soldiers

There were about 7,000 soldiers based on the Antonine Wall. These required feeding, clothing and housing, and supplying with arms and armour, cooking and eating equipment, medicines and bandages, and so on. Some of these items such as building stone and timber could be obtained locally. Others, however, came from further afield. The Antonine Wall was at the end of many long supply chains which stretched south into the province and across the Channel too.

Most grain probably had to be imported from elsewhere in Britain. Some cattle, however, appear to have been obtained locally. This is indicated by the bones which were of adult and well-grown animals of the Celtic short-horn variety. As we have seen, specialist items of food were imported from the Continent (see page 72).

Pottery for cooking and eating was mainly imported from southern Britain and Gaul, modern France. At least one potter, Sarrius, however, was adventurous enough to establish a workshop on the Wall. Somewhere in the vicinity of Bearsden he made mixing bowls for the troops in the fort.

Later in the history of the Roman empire, we know of factories making arms and armour, and it is possible that these were already in existence during the life of the Antonine Wall. A new recruit would have to buy his own arms and armour, and a share of his tent, when he joined the army. Later, deductions were made for hay, food, boots and socks, clothing and the camp Saturnalia dinner on 17 December. It is not surprising, therefore, that soldiers asked their families to send them specific items. Many letters record that clothing, including socks and underpants, sandals, arms and food were sent to soldiers. Sometimes, soldiers simply took these items for themselves from the local people.

This scene on Trajan's Column shows a ship being loaded with tents for transport along the River Danube

LIFE ON THE FRONTIER

Every army had its camp followers and the Roman army was no different. We might expect that there was a village outside every fort along the frontier where the soldiers' dependants lived. Here, also, there would have been inns, shops, temples and so on. Excavations on the Antonine Wall have revealed but scanty remains of such buildings. Recently, geophysical survey has been used to seek traces of civil settlements, but with little success.

Remains of field systems have been found outside several other forts. One is still visible to the east of the fort at Rough Castle. This consists of small plots bounded by earthen banks. The size of the plots is more suited to horticulture than farming, so perhaps vegetables were grown here. A metalled road passing through the field system, and leading towards the Military Way, may suggest a Roman date for the complex.

Aerial photography and geophysical survey have revealed another field system at Carriden, at the eastern end of the Wall. An altar found here in 1956 was erected by Aelius Mansuetus on behalf of the villagers settled at Fort Velunia (or Veluniate) and indicates that there was a form of community organisation there.

The people living in the civil settlement were dependent upon the soldiers, and many of them would have been their wives, children or other relatives. All were bound together, and when the regiment moved on, the people of the civil settlement would have packed up their belongings and moved too.

Religion

The Romans were eclectic in the gods they worshipped. They sought the blessing of individual gods: Jupiter for the well-being of the emperor; Mars for war; Silvanus for hunting; the gods of the neighbourhood for everyday life. Prior to any undertaking, a promise was made to the god: in return for success in the forthcoming venture, a gift would be offered to the deity. An altar would be dedicated, a bull sacrificed, a gift given, a dedication made ...

Some gods were official, the special gods of the Roman state. It was to Jupiter that each regiment of the Roman army paid a vow at the beginning of each year for the welfare of the emperor and for the eternity of the empire. Prayers to the gods were also said on the anniversary of the emperor's accession – 10 July in the case of Antoninus Pius. This date, and the birthday of the emperor, 19 September, were still being celebrated a hundred years later.

Not surprisingly, Mars was favoured by soldiers based on the Antonine Wall, altars being dedicated to the god at three forts. Surprisingly, the one dedication to Neptune was at Castlecary, one of the furthest forts from the sea. There is a dedication to Mercury here, on an altar which records the erection of a shrine to the god (see page 11). Hercules was favoured by an altar and a statue at Mumrills. Dedications to Fortuna are often found in bath-houses for she protected men when they were in their most vulnerable state, which is when they had no clothes on (see page 71).

The dedications can tell us a lot about the dedicator. Marcus Cocceius Firmus, a centurion of the Second Legion, dedicated four altars at Auchendavy to as many as ten gods (see page 119). Analysis of these suggests that he was born in a frontier province, probably on the Lower Danube, and had seen service in the emperor's mounted bodyguard in Rome before being promoted to centurion and at some stage posted to Britain.

A statue of Mars (partially restored) found at Balmuildy

Death on the frontier

Death was ever present on the Antonine Wall. It has been calculated that of any one intake of recruits about half their number would die in service. Death took many forms: fighting was only one. The dead were normally cremated and buried in the cemetery. Roman law forbade burial in built-up areas, so the cemetery was usually some distance from the fort.

A soldier buried at Croy appears to have been a member of a military family. The elderly soldier in the centre, sporting a full beard, is a legionary. This is clear from the rectangular and curved shape of his shield and his *pilum*, the special spear used by legionaries; his helmet is dangling on his shield. He is flanked by two younger legionaries, presumably his sons. Four inscriptions record the presence of soldiers of the Sixth Legion at this fort, and the tombstone may record the death of one of them.

Another cemetery lay at Shirva, between the forts of Bar Hill and Auchendavy. Tombstones and other funerary monuments were found here in 1728–9. The tombstones are of both soldiers and civilians. Buried here were Flavius Lucianus of the Second Legion and an unnamed soldier holding a box which shows that he had been promoted from the ranks. The civilians were fifteen-year-old Salmanes and a lady, Verecunda. Two stones depict different stages on the journey to the underworld. One shows a funeral banquet and the other a lady in a carriage drawn by two mules. These probably formed part of a larger monument, perhaps commemorating the wife of the commanding officer. These stones, together with a plaque of the Second Legion, were all reused in a later structure, probably a souterrain, built in the Antonine Wall ditch.

The purpose of the Antonine Wall

It is essential to study the Antonine Wall in its landscape setting to be able to understand its purpose. There are several places where the Wall does not take the best line – the best line, that is, if its primary purpose was military defence. Along the eastern 7 km (4½ miles) it ran along a raised beach overlooking the Firth of Forth. It did not, however, stand on the very edge of the escarpment, utilising the natural defence to the north, but lay a little distance to the south. Over Croy Hill, a nose of land was left to the north of the Wall (see page 14). The land in front of the rampart and ditch rose slightly to the north for 300 m before dropping sharply into the Kelvin Valley. For a little extra effort, the Wall could have been swung north to embrace this high point, but this was not done.

At the very west end of the Antonine Wall the earthworks were laid out across the slope with the land rising to the north from immediately in front of the ditch: the land continues to rise to create the spectacular Kilpatrick Braes. Clearly the Romans judged something else more important than placing the Wall in the best defensive position; this may have been a wish to protect the fording points over the River Clyde. Military defence would not appear to have been their main concern.

These three particular landscape observations lend support to the view that the primary purpose of the Antonine Wall was not military defence, but rather a demarcation line, intended to aid the task of frontier control.

The Kilpatrick Braes from the Antonine Wall

The end of the Wall

The Antonine Wall had a short life. Most of the evidence combines to suggest abandonment in the 160s, just a generation after it had been constructed. We do not know the reasons for this. Perhaps troops were required elsewhere – we certainly do know that British regiments were serving in Germany and probably also Africa at this time. Possibly the emperor and his advisors reviewed imperial commitments and decided to withdraw to Hadrian's Wall.

An inscription found on Hadrian's Wall, but now lost, records rebuilding in 158, the same year that similar work was underway at the fort at Birrens between the two Walls. If this was the start of the withdrawal, it extended over several years because a "fairly worn" coin of the Empress Lucilla, wife of the Emperor Lucius Verus, minted between 164 and 169, was found in the granary at Old Kilpatrick during excavations in the early 1920s.

The buildings in the forts on the Antonine Wall were demolished and burnt. Excavations at the fort at Bearsden in the 1970s revealed drains choked with burnt wattle and daub from timber buildings. The hand of the Roman army did not extend to the destruction of either the fort ramparts or the Antonine Wall rampart, as the survival of earthworks today demonstrates.

Three distance slabs have been found in circumstances, for example in a shallow pit, that suggest deliberate concealment. It is likely that the distance slabs were all taken down and buried when the Antonine Wall was abandoned. Other important items were also hidden. At Bar Hill, an altar and commemorative plaque were dropped into the well together with architectural fragments from the headquarters building.

The death of Antoninus Pius

Antoninus Pius died as the Antonine Wall was being abandoned. This occurred on 7 March 161 when he was in his seventy-fifth year. As befitting a man who preferred home comforts to the trappings of imperial power, he died at his childhood home, his villa at Lorium, 20 km (13 miles) west of Rome.

The body of Antoninus Pius was cremated on the Campus Martius in Rome and buried in the great mausoleum built by Hadrian, now known as Castel Sant'Angelo. In fact, Antoninus had completed the building of the mausoleum at the beginning of his reign, and it was called the *Antoninorum sepulcrum*, the burial place of the Antonines. The ashes of his wife, his sons and his daughter had previously been placed within it.

The successors of Antoninus Pius, Marcus Aurelius and Lucius Verus, erected a column beside the funeral pyre. This later fell and was buried, to be rediscovered in 1703 beside the Via di Campo Marzio. The column itself was used to repair the obelisk now standing in the Piazza Montecitorio. The base of the Column of Antoninus was taken to the Vatican Museum where it still is. On one side of the base is a vision of Antoninus and his wife Faustina ascending to heaven.

Faustina had died many years before, in 141. A temple had then been erected in her honour in the Forum in Rome; on the death of Antoninus, it was rededicated to the imperial couple. In the Middle Ages it was turned into a church and we owe its survival to this act.

The base of the Column of Antoninus Pius

*The temple of Antoninus and Faustina
in the Forum, Rome*

Coin showing the funeral pyre of Antoninus Pius

Keeping in with the locals

The abandonment of the Antonine Wall did not end Roman interest in the land to the north of Hadrian's Wall. In 197, and again in 367, we are informed by Roman writers of treaties between Rome and its northern neighbours in Britain. In 197, the treaty was described as being with the Caledonians and the Maeatae. At that time, in order to keep the peace, the governor of Britain paid "a considerable sum" to the Maeatae, receiving in turn a few prisoners. The Maeatae, we believe, lived north of the eastern end of the Antonine Wall.

It was an established part of Roman diplomacy to interfere in the affairs of states beyond their boundaries in order to maintain a situation which was in their favour. They supported pro-Roman kings and encouraged the deposition – and murder – of others. Their support was underpinned by gifts. Such gifts might be artefacts or coins. Many coin hoards are known from north Britain beyond Hadrian's Wall. One such hoard was found at Falkirk, close to the abandoned Antonine Wall. It contained 2,000 silver coins – *denarii* – ranging in date from 83 BC to AD 230. Nearly every emperor from Nero, who reigned from 54 to 68, to Severus Alexander, emperor from 222 to 235, is represented in the hoard, suggesting that it was built up over several generations.

The Turriff jug

This complete glass vessel was found near Turriff in Aberdeenshire between 1855 and 1857, during the construction of a railway line. It is made from blown green glass, with a long neck and diagonal ribbing on the body. It dates to the second century AD.

It is rare to find such fine glass vessels complete and unbroken. When they are found complete, they are normally recovered from burials. In this case, the only information we have is that the jug was found in a sandy hillock together with many glass beads, none of which survive.

In the circumstances, it is only possible to speculate about the way in which this jug arrived so far north of the Roman frontier. Possibly it was a gift to a local chief or king. Perhaps a returning soldier had brought it back with him. Although no Caledonian is known to have joined the Roman army, this is not a fanciful possibility as recruits for the Roman army were drawn from beyond other frontiers. A Caledonian, Lossio Veda by name, is known from within the province: he dedicated a votive plaque at Colchester during the reign of the Emperor Severus Alexander (222–35). Most of the Roman material found north of the frontier lies relatively close to the coast, suggesting that it had travelled there by sea.

Later use of the Antonine Wall

The earthworks of the Wall saved several later castle builders some trouble as it already provided a raised platform for them. No less than five castles lie on the earthworks of the Antonine Wall. They include one stone-built structure, Inveravon Tower, and several mottes, mounds of earth on which would have sat a timber tower. These lay at Watling Lodge, Seabegs and Cadder. The motte at Watling Lodge, called Maiden Castle, sat on the upcast mound and was destroyed in 1894, when the present house was built. The motte at Seabegs stands in the grounds of Antonine Primary School in Bonnybridge.

The most impressive surviving castle remains today are at Kirkintilloch. Lying on the line of the Antonine Wall, and for centuries believed to be a Roman fort, we now appreciate that the surviving earthworks are medieval in date. King William the Lion made Kirkintilloch into a burgh of barony in 1170, and it is possible that this was the castle of the then laird, William Cumin. The castle was lost to the Cumin or Comyn family when Robert the Bruce seized the throne in 1306.

Today, the remains of this castle are a large mound surrounded by a substantial ditch, lying in Peel Park, which itself has been extensively landscaped. Nevertheless, signs of rig and furrow cultivation can still be seen on the north slopes below the position of the Antonine Wall, which is marked out in the park.

Modern land-use

The Antonine Wall runs through a diverse landscape. As we have seen, it utilises the terrain well, be it the valleys of the Rivers Carron and Kelvin and drumlins north of Glasgow or the raised beach alongside the Forth. Its underlying geology is equally mixed, from sands and clays to hard volcanic dolerite. These soils and rocks affected the nature of the frontier itself.

This landscape is now overlain by the activities of farmers and industrialists, quarriers and builders. Historic Scotland and the Royal Commission on the Ancient and Historical Monuments of Scotland have been mapping the historic land-use of Scotland. This is a long process that will take several years to complete. The area of the Antonine Wall has already been assessed and mapped.

In the countryside, the predominant field pattern dates to the years following the improvements which took place during the Agricultural Revolution of the eighteenth century. In some areas the road pattern of that date also remains. This is especially clear in the area between the Wall and Kilsyth. While modern roads stride across the countryside north of Cumbernauld, linking new housing estates, the smaller roads of an earlier period can still be recognised between Dullatur and Twechar in particular. Here too can be seen the landscaping undertaken by the local landowners, the Whitelaws of Gartshore, in the late nineteenth century. Yet, in spite of these changes, pockets relating to earlier activities, such as the Antonine Wall, survive, as do other relics of the former use of the land, pit heaps and quarries.

    Historic land-use map of the area between Twechar and Dullatur

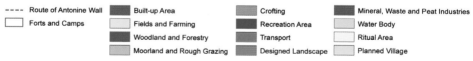

- - - - Route of Antonine Wall
☐ Forts and Camps

■ Built-up Area
☐ Fields and Farming
■ Woodland and Forestry
■ Moorland and Rough Grazing

■ Crofting
■ Recreation Area
■ Transport
■ Designed Landscape

■ Mineral, Waste and Peat Industries
■ Water Body
☐ Ritual Area
☐ Planned Village

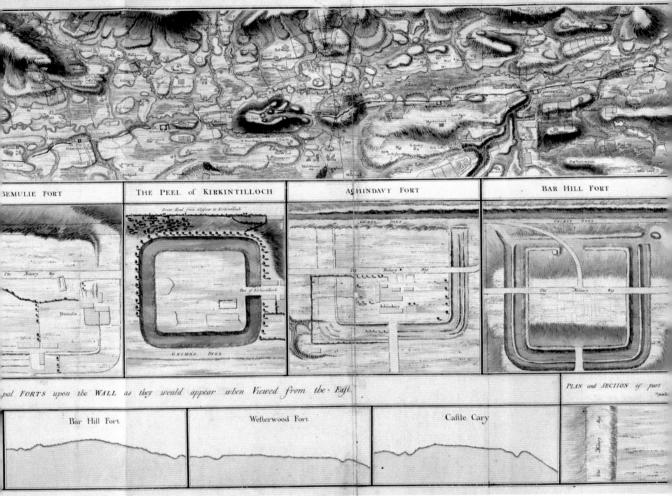

veen the *FORTH* and the *CLYDE*, in the Reign of **ANTONINUS PIUS** by Lollius Urbicus *then Commanding the* **ROMAN FORCES** *in*

BEMULIE FORT   THE PEEL of KIRKINTILLOCH   ACHINDAVY FORT   BAR HILL FORT

pal FORTS upon the WALL as they would appear when Viewed from the East.   PLAN and SECTION of part

Bar Hill Fort   Wefterwood Fort   Caftle Cary

Mapping the Antonine Wall

Matthew Paris' thirteenth-century map of Britain shows two Roman frontiers across northern Britain, as indeed there were. The scale of the depiction precludes any detail. More illuminating is Timothy Pont's sixteenth-century map. On this, the Wall can be traced from Kilpatrick on the Clyde, almost to its eastern terminus. The Wall passed through places where it is still to be recognised, such as Dunotyr, Barhill, Croy, Dulettyr, Mumrels and Castel Cary.

Our next significant map is that prepared by William Roy. A Scot from Carluke, Roy was employed by the British army in the aftermath of the Jacobite Uprising of 1745/6 to map Scotland. He soon discovered an interest in the earlier Roman fortifications. As he noted, "military men . . . are naturally led to compare present things with the past". In 1755, he surveyed the Antonine Wall, producing a map of the whole monument, locating not only the rampart and ditch, but also the Military Way and the forts, and he recorded inscriptions and other objects from the Wall. His map was remarkably accurate and was not surpassed until the Ordnance Survey's work a century later.

Roy died in 1790 and his map was subsequently published in 1793 in a monumental work, *The Military Antiquities of the Romans in Britain*. Another posthumous gift to his country was the foundation of the Ordnance Survey, the inspiration of Roy and the culmination of his long military service.

The Antonine Wall bears a monument to the achievements of William Roy. On Castle Hill, next to Bar Hill, sits a trig point, used by the Ordnance Survey to aid the survey of the area, but no longer required and so now maintained by Historic Scotland (see pages 28–29).

Modern mapping

The Ordnance Survey has continued the tradition of mapping the Antonine Wall. Its last complete survey was in 1980. Since that date, its archaeological role has been taken over by the Royal Commission on the Ancient and Historical Monuments of Scotland. This body records new excavations on the Antonine Wall and annotates its maps accordingly. Sometimes minor shifts in the depicted line of the Wall are required.

New information comes not just through archaeological excavations but also through aerial archaeology. The late 1940s saw the value of this new tool, with fortlets and camps being discovered on the Wall. Much of the Wall, however, lies in pasture and therefore rarely reveals buried archaeological features to the aerial surveyor. The crop marks defining one of the construction camps on the Antonine Wall are shown on page 38.

Over the last decades, a new tool has come to the aid of archaeologists – geophysical survey. This records differences in soil and moisture conditions and thereby can allow the planning of lost features. On the Antonine Wall, such survey has revealed the circuit of fort defences, but it is not helpful in tracing minor structural elements like post-holes. As many buildings in forts were of timber, with their uprights in individual post-holes, geophysical survey has limitations on the Antonine Wall.

The combined use of different techniques can be informative about the frontier installations. The fort at Balmuildy has been plotted by the Ordnance Survey, excavated and planned by archaeologists, recorded by aerial surveyors, and most recently surveyed through geophysics. In spite of its prior excavation, the geophysical survey was able to produce new evidence.

A geophysical plan of Balmuildy fort prepared by Glasgow University

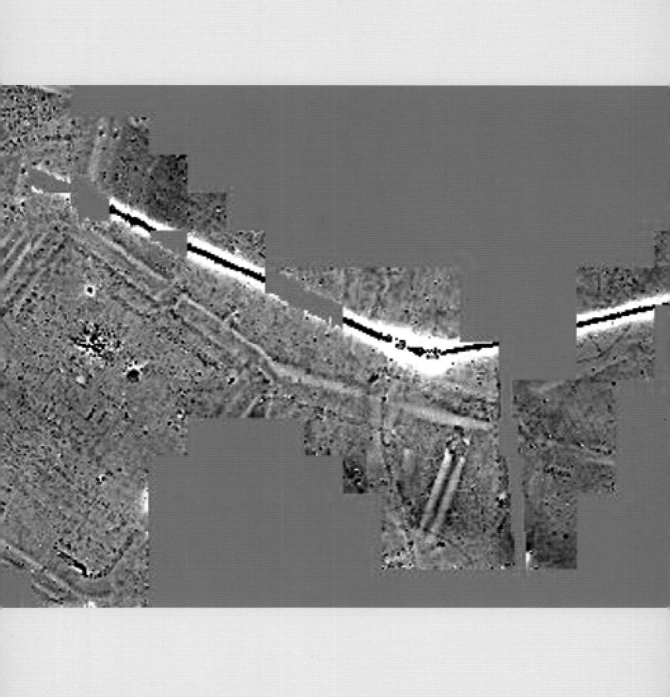

LATRINE, & ADJOINING FOUNDATION OF NORTH WALL.

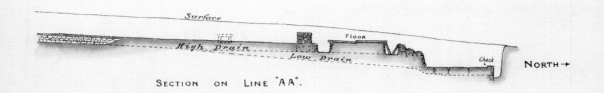

Surface

High Drain

Floor

Low Drain

Check

NORTH →

SECTION ON LINE "AA".

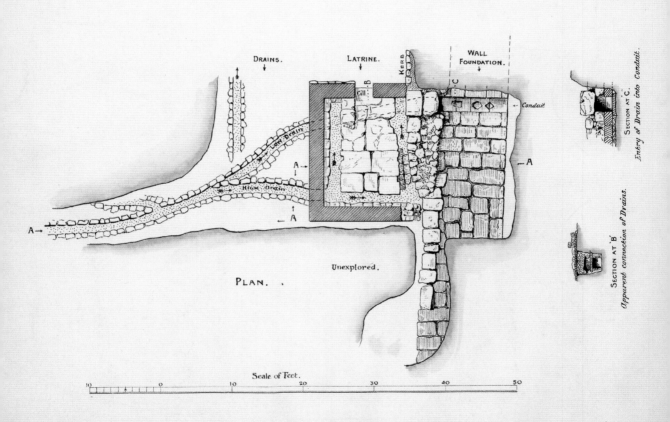

DRAINS.

LATRINE.

KERB

WALL FOUNDATION.

B

Gill

Low Drain

C

Conduit

A →

A →

↓
A →

High Drain

A

← A

A →

Section at C.
Entry of Drain into Conduit.

Section at B.
Apparent connection of Drains.

Unexplored.

PLAN.

Scale of Feet.

10   0   10   20   30   40   50

Rediscovering the Antonine Wall

Antiquarians and other visitors to the Antonine Wall have been recording its remains since the sixteenth century, pondering the significance of their observations. In the nineteenth century, scholars turned from merely mapping and recording the Wall to excavation. In the 1890s, the Glasgow Archaeological Society investigated the nature of the rampart and ditch, while the Society of Antiquaries of Scotland concentrated on forts, examining Castlecary in 1902 and Rough Castle in 1902–3. Rescue excavations started about the same time, with the fortlet at Watling Lodge being examined in 1894 prior to a new villa being constructed. Excavations on the Antonine Wall continue to this day.

Periodically, general overviews have been produced. These include Sir George Macdonald's magisterial *The Roman Wall in Scotland*, the second edition of which was produced in 1934. Bill Hanson and Gordon Maxwell published a modern account in 1986, *Rome's North-West Frontier, The Antonine Wall*. The other indispensable book is Anne Robertson's guide, *The Antonine Wall*, first published in 1960, with the account of the monument and the bibliography regularly updated by Lawrence Keppie.

This plan of the latrine at Castlecary was drawn by Mungo Buchanan during the excavations in 1902

The Antonine Wall in popular culture

As Scotland moved into the modern age in the eighteenth century and the Wall came under pressure from agricultural improvements, industry and population growth, interest in the country's Roman antiquities remained strong. Glasgow University started collecting Roman inscriptions from the Antonine Wall in the seventeenth century, and they came to form an important part of the Hunterian Museum, founded in Glasgow in 1807. To the east, the museum of the Society of Antiquaries of Scotland, established in 1780, now forms a vital element within the National Museum of Scotland in Edinburgh. The Roman altars, sculpture and other artefacts from the Antonine Wall still receive pride of place in the displays of these two important museums.

Scotland's Roman past was also acknowledged in another fashion. Antoninus Pius and his general Lollius Urbicus appeared on the frieze of Scottish heroes, created in the 1880s, in the Scottish National Portrait Gallery. At the beginning of the twentieth century a stained-glass window in Kirkintilloch's new town hall depicted a Roman soldier standing beside the Antonine Wall. The same burgh's coat-of-arms includes the gate of the Roman fort at Kirkintilloch. Now, the Antonine Wall is more likely to be acknowledged through the names of streets and housing developments. These include Roman Road and Antonine Court in Bearsden, as well as the Roman Bar in Falkirk.

*The coat-of-arms of Kirkintilloch, a stained-glass window of a Roman soldier formerly
in Kirkintilloch Town Hall, and the frieze in the Scottish National Portrait Gallery*

Re-enactment

All periods of history now seem to have their re-enactment groups. One of the oldest and most respected of such groups is the Ermine Street Guard, formed in 1972. It regularly gives demonstrations of drill and equipment in Britain and abroad.

Here the centurion marches at the head of his men, with the *vexillarius* carrying the *vexillum* (flag) of the Twentieth Legion and the *imaginifer* bearing the image of the emperor; the standards are garlanded in celebration of the Roman festival of *Floralia* held each year from 28 April to 3 May. Behind are legionaries, while at the rear are several auxiliary soldiers.

In Scotland, a special re-enactment group, the Antonine Guard, was formed in 1990. It consists of two sections, a detachment of the Sixth Legion and one of the Sixth Cohort of Nervians and First Cohort of Hamians.

Roads and tracks

Even where the Antonine Wall is no longer visible as a surface feature, its line can often still be recognised. This is because the Military Way sometimes continued in use as a road, as in Bearsden, where Roman Road lies on top of its 1,800-year-old predecessor. Elsewhere, roads and tracks follow the line of the rampart or ditch. In Bo'ness, Dean Road and Grahamsdyke Road lie on the ditch and the line continues westward to form the drive leading to Kinneil House. Grahamsdyke Street in Laurieston lies mainly on the upcast mound. Further west, Arnothill Road in Falkirk marks the line of the Wall. In Duntocher the line of the Wall is left open alongside Beeches Avenue, while the track running westwards from the end of the modern road lies beside the Wall.

The names of these roads often record their associations. 'Grahamsdyke' reflects the name previously given to the Antonine Wall – Grim's Dyke. This name can be traced as far back as the fourteenth century, when the historian John of Fordoun stated that it was called 'Grymisdyke' because it had been destroyed by Gryme, grandfather of King Eugenius, both, alas, mythical figures. George Buchanan, tutor to King James VI in the sixteenth century, offered another explanation. Graeme was a leader of the Picts and Scots who broke down the Wall from the south so that his countrymen could invade the Roman province. The real derivation of the name, however, may be more prosaic. The Gaelic word *grym* means strong.

Visibility analysis

Modern computer techniques enable us to understand the Antonine Wall in its setting as never before. While preparing its recommendations for the definition of the buffer zones for the nomination of the Antonine Wall as a World Heritage Site, Land Use Consultants undertook a visibility analysis. This was based on "bare-ground terrain data", that is, it was based on the modern ground surface; trees and buildings, which would screen views, were ignored. Nevertheless, the results of the analysis were valuable. They demonstrated that, in general, clear visibility extended to within 1 km (less than a mile) of the Wall; beyond this, the land forms impaired visibility. Longer distance views tend to be northwards: on this map the darker areas are those with greater intervisibility between the Wall and the surrounding countryside. These include not only the Campsie Fells, but the river valleys. The exception to this is the west end of the frontier, where the views to the north are limited, while those to the south are extensive.

More detailed analysis can demonstrate intervisibility along the line of the Wall. "View-shed analysis" can indicate what can be seen from any one point on the frontier. This can be of value not only in aiding understanding of how the Wall worked, but also in seeking hitherto undiscovered sites which might be considered to exist because they covered locations out of visual contact with other forts or fortlets.

Map indicating the levels of visibility from the Antonine Wall;
the darker areas are more visible from the Wall

Firth of Clyde

Firth of Forth

Glasgow

The protection of the Antonine Wall

The first steps to protect the Antonine Wall occurred in 1926, when several sections were scheduled as ancient monuments under the Ancient Monuments Act 1913. Now 40 km (24 miles) – exactly two-thirds of the whole monument – is scheduled. The remaining one-third of the Antonine Wall, lying under the towns and villages along its line, is protected under the Town and Country Planning (Scotland) Act 1997. These two Acts of Parliament provide sufficient protection for the whole of the Antonine Wall, including all its ancillary features, within the proposed World Heritage Site.

UNESCO requires that every World Heritage Site is protected by a buffer zone. In 1957, the first steps were taken to protect the environs of the Antonine Wall through the definition of amenity zones. The aim was not just to protect the amenity of the Antonine Wall, but to preserve, so far as is possible, this unique linear monument within swathes of undeveloped countryside so that it could be better understood. It was appreciated that if the ground were to be developed up to the limits of the protected archaeology, it would become impossible to view the monument as a whole or to gain any understanding of the topographical appreciation made by the Roman surveyors. Indeed, the very purpose of the frontier can only be understood by seeing it within its wider landscape setting. In 2006, a review of the environs of the Antonine Wall was undertaken by Land Use Consultants and buffer zones defined for the proposed World Heritage Site.

An historic event. The then Minister for Tourism, Culture and Sport, Patricia Ferguson, MSP, together with representatives of East Dunbartonshire, Falkirk, the City of Glasgow, North Lanarkshire and West Dunbartonshire Councils, signs a Concordat on 20 June 2006 for the better protection of the Antonine Wall

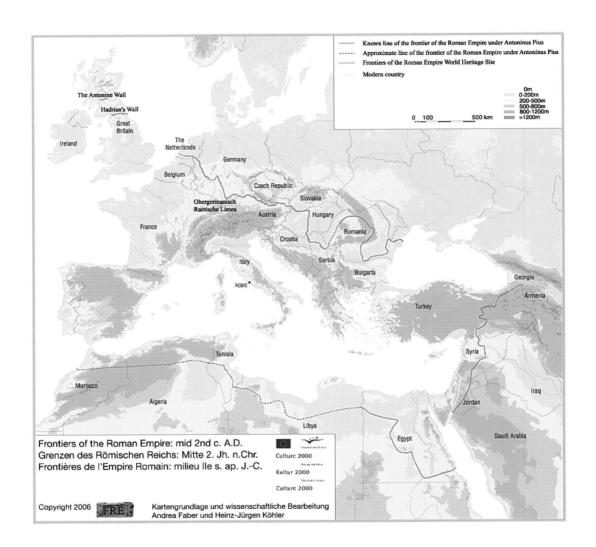

Frontiers of the Roman Empire: mid 2nd c. A.D.
Grenzen des Römischen Reichs: Mitte 2. Jh. n.Chr.
Frontières de l'Empire Romain: milieu IIe s. ap. J.-C.

Culture 2000
Kultur 2000
Culture 2000

Copyright 2006 FRE

Kartengrundlage und wissenschaftliche Bearbeitung
Andrea Faber und Heinz-Jürgen Köhler

Legend items:
Known line of the frontier of the Roman Empire under Antoninus Pius
Approximate line of the frontier of the Roman Empire under Antoninus Pius
Frontiers of the Roman Empire World Heritage Site
Modern country

0m
0-200m
200-500m
500-800m
800-1200m
>1200m

0   100   500 km

The Antonine Wall in its international context

The Romans tended to use natural features to define the edge of their empire: rivers, mountains and deserts. Where none existed, they might erect an artificial frontier. The Antonine Wall was one such frontier, for a short time replacing Hadrian's Wall as the northern frontier of the province of Britain. In Germany, a frontier of timber was erected at about the same time as Hadrian's Wall. This was moved forward and replaced by a new frontier about the same time that the Antonine Wall was abandoned.

In 2005, Hadrian's Wall, a World Heritage Site since 1987, combined with the newly ascribed German frontier, to form a new World Heritage Site, Frontiers of the Roman Empire. In summer 2008, the World Heritage Committee will decide whether the Antonine Wall should be added to this World Heritage Site.

These three artificial frontiers in western Europe are not the only linear barriers on the borders of the Roman empire. Passes in Dacia, modern Romania, were often closed by short lengths of rampart and ditch. In North Africa, a wall, together with towers and forts, protected the cultivated ground from the movement of nomads: this was the *Fossatum Africae*.

Work is in progress in many countries to prepare cases for the Frontiers of the Roman Empire World Heritage Site to be extended. If successful, a truly unique World Heritage Site will be created, balancing the great cities and monuments within the frontiers of the former Roman empire which are already World Heritage Sites including, of course, Rome itself.

The future

Although research has been undertaken on the Antonine Wall for centuries, it still retains a capacity to surprise. The discovery of fortlets in the 1940s changed our perception of the frontier. In 1975, a suggestion that there had originally been a fortlet at roughly every mile along its length led to the discovery of a further five sites, bringing the tally to nine. Also in the 1970s, Gordon Maxwell, while examining aerial photographs, recognised the existence of three small enclosures attached to the rear of the Wall at Wilderness Plantation.

Temporary camps came to be found along the Antonine Wall through aerial survey in the 1940s and 1950s. We now know of as many as twenty. Several have now been excavated and some have demonstrated more than one period of use, which was a surprising discovery.

Some new discoveries are the result of serendipity. These include the identification in breaks in the stone base of the Antonine Wall, probably indicating the work of different legions, and the finding of pits on the berm, that is between the rampart and the ditch. A further surprise is that archaeological remains of the Antonine Wall survive as well in the towns and villages along the Wall as in the countryside. In both Bearsden and Falkirk the long-lost forts have been located and partially planned. Elsewhere, a bath-house has been found in Callendar Park, Falkirk, while the rampart base survives intact through much of the town. It is for this reason, as well as to emphasise the linearity of the frontier, that the area proposed as a World Heritage Site includes those stretches of the Wall in urban contexts as well as the rural environment.

If there is one thing that is certain, it is that more discoveries will come to light which will challenge our current beliefs in the building and history of the Antonine Wall.

The children of Antonine Primary School in Bonnybridge prepare to do battle with a member of the Antonine Guard

Finding the Antonine Wall

The following places are the best locations to see the Antonine Wall:

Best lengths of rampart and ditch: Rough Castle and Seabegs Wood, both in Bonnybridge

Best ditch: Watling Lodge, Callendar Park and Polmont in Falkirk; Garnhall and Tollpark near Castlecary; Croy Hill and Bar Hill near Kilsyth

Rampart base: New Kilpatrick Cemetery and Roman Park in Bearsden; Golden Hill in Duntocher; Kemper Avenue, Falkirk

Military Way: Rough Castle (where there are also quarry pits) and Seabegs Wood, both in Bonnybridge

Forts: Rough Castle, where there are also the *lilia*; Bar Hill, where the headquarters building and bath-house are laid out for inspection; Castlecary, where some stonework of the east fort wall and at the headquarters building can be seen; and Duntocher, where the line of the ditch and part of the rampart base are marked. The sites of the forts on Croy Hill and in Peel Park, Kirkintilloch, are in public ownership, though no archaeological remains are visible

Bath-houses: Bearsden and Bar Hill

Fortlet: Kinneil in Bo'ness

Expansions: Rough Castle and Croy Hill

End of the Wall: the east end of the Antonine Wall is marked at Bo'ness by a copy of the inscription from the Bridgeness distance slab

Best walk: Castlecary Hotel to Twechar through Tollpark and Westerwood and over Croy Hill and Bar Hill

Roman Park, Bearsden, from the air. This stretch of the Wall survives in the middle of a modern housing estate.

MUSEUMS

The finds from the Antonine Wall are housed in several museums along the Wall line. **The Hunterian Museum** in the University of Glasgow has seventeen of the known twenty distance slabs and many artefacts from the Wall, including those from the well at Bar Hill. A new Antonine Wall Centre devoted to the Roman material and providing an information focus for visitors to the Antonine Wall and Roman Scotland will be opened in the Hunterian Museum in 2008. The museum is home to the Antonine Wall archive.

Website: **www.hunterian.gla.ac.uk**   Email: **hunter@museum.gla.ac.uk**

The National Museum of Scotland in Edinburgh is home to the most easterly distance slab found, the Bridgeness Stone, and artefacts from the forts in the eastern half of the frontier.

Website: **www.nms.ac.uk**   Email: **info@nms.ac.uk**

There are two museums in Falkirk, both sitting beside the Antonine Wall. **Kinneil Museum** displays material from the fortlet, as well as the Kinneil estate. **Callendar House** in the centre of Falkirk has an exhibition primarily aimed at school children.

Website: **www.falkirk.gov.uk/cultural**   Email: **callendar.house@falkirk.gov.uk**

Auld Kirk Museum in Kirkintilloch contains an exhibition illustrating finds from the area. The Antonine Wall crosses Peel Park which lies beside the museum.

Website: **www.eastdunbarton.gov.uk**

An altar dedicated by Marcus Cocceius Firmus at Auchendavy, now in the Hunterian Museum

ARCHIVES

The Royal Commission on the Ancient and Historical Monuments of Scotland,
John Sinclair House, 16 Bernard Terrace, Edinburgh, holds a national collection of
information and archive about Scotland's architectural and archaeological heritage,
which includes many records relating to the Antonine Wall. Its database, Canmore, is
available on-line at: **www.rcahms.gov.uk**

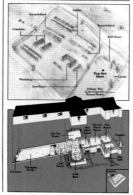
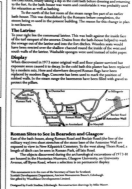

The two local Sites and Monuments Records for the Antonine Wall are:

Falkirk Museum, Callendar House, Callendar Park, Falkirk FK1 1YR
Email: **geoff.bailey@falkirk.gov.uk**

West of Scotland Archaeology Service, 20 India Street, Glasgow G2 4PF
Website: **www.wosas.net**   Email: **enquiries@wosas.glasgow.gov.uk**

PHOTOGRAPHS

The photographs in this book are available from the following four bodies:
Historic Scotland: hs.images@scotland.gsi.gov.uk
Hunterian Museum, University of Glasgow: photolibrary@museum.gla.ac.uk
National Museums of Scotland: info@nms.ac.uk
Royal Commission on the Ancient and Historical Monuments of Scotland:
www.rcahms.gov.uk/order.html

Modern interpretation ranges from on-site notice boards
to school visits to museum displays

FURTHER READING

The Antonine Wall

Bailey, G. B., *The Antonine Wall: Rome's Northern Frontier* (Falkirk, 2003)

Birley, E., *Roman Britain and the Roman Army* (Kendal, 1961)

Breeze, D. J., *The Antonine Wall* (Edinburgh, 2006)

Breeze, D. J. and Dobson, B., *Hadrian's Wall*, 4th ed. (London, 2000)

Hanson, W. S. and Maxwell, G. S., *Rome's North-west Frontier: the Antonine Wall* (Edinburgh, 1986)

Keppie, L. J. F., *Roman Inscribed and Sculptured Stones in the Hunterian Museum*, University of Glasgow (London, 1998)

Keppie, L., *The Legacy of Rome. Scotland's Roman Remains* (Edinburgh, 2004)

Macdonald, G., *The Roman Wall in Scotland* (London, 1934)

Robertson, A .S., *The Antonine Wall*, rev. ed. by Keppie, L .J. F. (Glasgow, 2001): this contains a full bibliography relating to the Antonine Wall

Roy, W., *The Military Antiquities of the Romans in Britain* (London, 1793)

Skinner, D. N., *The Countryside of the Antonine Wall* (Perth, 1973)

Woolliscroft, D. J., *Roman Military Signalling* (London, 2001)

Reports on excavations are generally published in one of the following journals:
Proceedings of the Society of Antiquaries of Scotland; Scottish Archaeological Journal or *Britannia.*

Roman Scotland

Breeze, D. J., *Roman Scotland: Frontier Country* (London, 2006)

Hunter, F., *Beyond the Edge of the Empire – Caledonians, Picts and Romans* (Rosemarkie, 2007)

Maxwell, G. S., *The Romans in Scotland* (Edinburgh, 1989)

Antoninus Pius

Lives of the later Caesars (Historia Augusta),
translated by Birley, A. (London, 1976)

Birley, A.R., *Marcus Aurelius* (London,
1987)

Frontiers of the Roman Empire
World Heritage Site

Breeze, D. J., *The Antonine Wall,
The North-West Frontier of the Roman
Empire, Proposed as a World Heritage
Site* (Edinburgh, 2004) describes the
proposal to make the Antonine Wall a
World Heritage Site

Breeze, D. J., Jilek, S. and Thiel,
A., *Frontiers of the Roman Empire*
(Edinburgh, Esslingen and Wien,
2005) sets the Antonine Wall in a
wider context

Frontiers and the Roman army

Austin, N. J. E. and Rankov, N.,
*Exploratio: Military and Political
Intelligence in the Roman World*
(London, 1995)

Brewer, R. (ed.), *The Second Augustan
Legion and the Roman Military Machine*
(Cardiff, 2002)

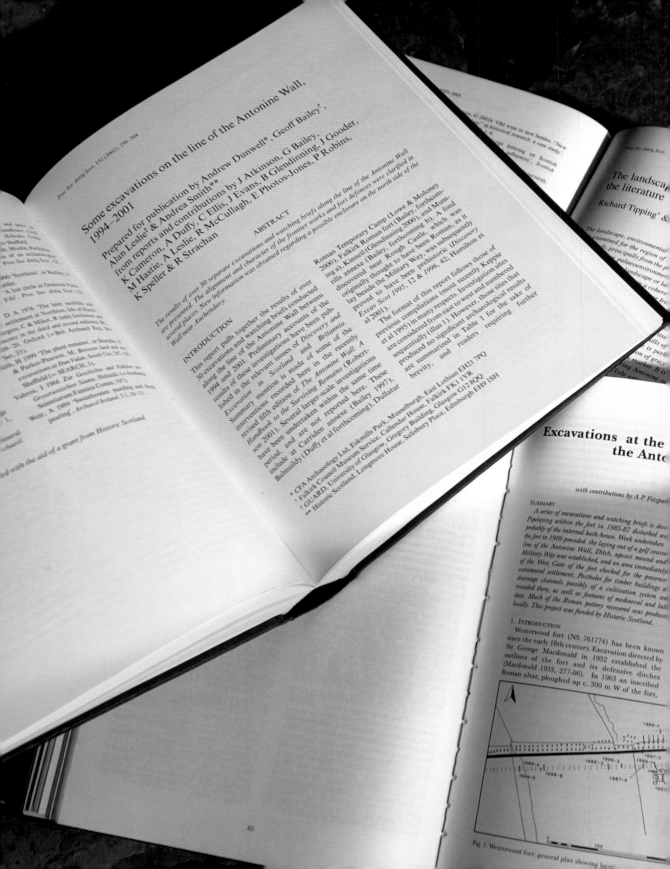

Proc Soc Antiq Scot, 132 (2002), 259–304

Some excavations on the line of the Antonine Wall, 1994–2001

Prepared for publication by Andrew Dunwell*, Geoff Bailey†,
Alan Leslie‡ & Andrea Smith**
from reports and contributions by J Atkinson, G Bailey,
K Cameron, A Duffy, C Ellis, J Evans, B Glendinning, J Gooder,
M Hastie, A Leslie, R McCullagh, E Photos-Jones, P Robins,
K Speller & R Strachan

ABSTRACT

The results of over 30 separate excavations and watching briefs along the line of the Antonine Wall are presented. The alignment and character of the frontier works and fort defences were clarified in several places. New information was obtained regarding a possible enclosure on the north side of the Wall near Auchendavy.

INTRODUCTION

This report pulls together the results of over 30 excavations and watching briefs conducted along the line of the Antonine Wall between 1994 and 2001. Preliminary accounts of the results of these investigations have been published in the relevant issues of *Discovery and Excavation in Scotland* and *Britannia*. Summary mention is made of some of the interventions recorded here in the recently revised fifth edition of *The Antonine Wall: A Handbook to the Surviving Remains* (Robertson 2001). Several larger-scale investigations have been undertaken within the same time period, and are not reported here. These include at Carriden annexe (Bailey 1997), Balmuildy (Duffy et al forthcoming), Dullatur

Roman Temporary Camp (Lowe & Moloney 2000), Falkirk Roman fort (Bailey, forthcoming a), Kinneil (Glendinning 2000), and Mumrills annexe (Bailey, forthcoming b). A ford discovered near Rough Castle, which was originally thought to have been Roman, as it lay beside the Military Way, was subsequently proved to have been prehistoric (*Discovery Excav Scot* 1995, 12 & 1996, 42; Hamilton et al 2001).

The format of this report follows those of previous compilations (most recently Keppie et al 1995) in many respects. Investigation sites are considered from east to west and numbered sequentially (illus 1). However, those sites that produced no significant archaeological results are summarized in Table 1 for the sake of brevity, and readers requiring further

* CFA Archaeology Ltd, Eskmills Park, Musselburgh, East Lothian EH21 7PQ
† Falkirk Council Museum Service, Callendar House, Callendar Park, Falkirk FK1 1YR
‡ GUARD, University of Glasgow, Gregory Building, Glasgow G12 8QQ
** Historic Scotland, Longmore House, Salisbury Place, Edinburgh EH9 1SH

Excavations at the ... the Ant...

with contributions by A P Fitzpat...

SUMMARY

A series of excavations and watching briefs is desc... Pipelaying within the fort in 1985–87 disturbed we... probably of the internal bath-house. Work undertaken ... the fort in 1986 preceded the laying out of a golf course ... line of the Antonine Wall, Ditch, upcast mound and ... Military Way was established, and an area immediately ... of the West Gate of the fort checked for the presence ... extramural settlement. Postholes for timber buildings a... drainage channels possibly of a cultivation system w... revealed there, as well as features of mediaeval and lat... date. Much of the Roman pottery recovered was produce... locally. This project was funded by Historic Scotland.

1. INTRODUCTION

Westerwood fort (NS 761774) has been known ... since the early 18th century. Excavation directed by ... Sir George Macdonald in 1932 established the ... outlines of the fort and its defensive ditches ... (Macdonald 1933, 277–86). In 1963 an inscribed ... Roman altar, ploughed up c. 300 m W of the fort, ...

Fig. 1 Westerwood fort, general plan showing locat...

Campbell, B., *The Roman Army, 31 BC – AD 337, A Sourcebook* (London, 1994)

Connolly, P., *Greece and Rome at War* (London, 1981)

Davies, R. W., *Service in the Roman Army*, ed. Breeze, D. J. and Maxfield V. A. (Edinburgh, 1989)

Erdcamp, P. (ed.), *A Companion to the Roman Army* (Oxford, 2007)

Ferris, I. M., *Enemies of Rome. Barbarians through Roman Eyes* (Stroud, 2000)

Goldsworthy, A., *The Complete Roman Army* (London, 2003)

Le Bohec, Y., *The Imperial Roman Army* (London and New York, 1994)

Luttwak, E. N., *The Grand Strategy of the Roman Empire* (Baltimore, 1976)

Mattern, S. P., *Rome and the Enemy. Imperial Strategy in the Principate* (Berkeley, Los Angeles and London, 1999)

Webster, G., *The Roman Imperial Army* (London, 1981)

Original sources

Most Roman sources for the history of Roman Britain are collected in:

Mann, J. C. and Penman, R. G., *Literary Sources for Roman Britain* (LACTOR 11, London, 1985)

Maxfield, V. A. and Dobson, B., *Inscriptions of Roman Britain* (LACTOR 4, London, 2006)

The Roman treatises on the army are translated:

Flavius Arrianus, *TEXNH TAKTIKA (Tactical handbook) AND EKTAI KATA ANΩN (The expedition against the Alans)*, translated and edited by DeVoto, J. G. (Chicago, 1993)

Josephus, *The Jewish War*, translated by Williamson, G. A. (Harmonsworth, 1959)

Polybius and Pseudo-Hyginus: *Fortification of the Roman Camp*, translated and edited by Miller, M. C. J. and DeVoto, J. G. (Chicago, 1994)

Vegetius: *Epitome of Military Science*, translated by Milner, N. P. (Liverpool, 1993)

Index

Acknowledgements and Picture Credits

I am grateful to Michelle Andersson, Geoff Bailey, Jim Devine, Brian Dobson, Richard Fawcett, George Findlater, Ben Harte, Fraser Hunter, Rebecca Jones, Lawrence Keppie, Lesley Macinnes and Richard Strachan for help in preparing this book and to Jackie Henrie for copy editing the manuscript with her usual skill. The map of the Antonine Wall on the end pages has been prepared by Leeanne Whitelaw of CFA Archaeology.

The illustrations are copyright: Auld Kirk Museum, Kirkintilloch (page 103 both top); Trustees of the British Museum (pages 2 and 16); the Culture 2000 Frontiers of the Roman Empire project, per Dr Sonja Jilek (page 112); the Ermine Street Guard (page 104); Department of Archaeology, University of Glasgow, per Dr Richard Jones (page 99); Historic Scotland (pages 6-8, 14, 28-9, 41, 42, 45, 46, 49, 54 top, 57, 61, 62, 63, 64, 70, 71, 76, 83, 84, 92, 95, 107, 109, 111, 115, 123, 124); Hunterian Museum, University of Glasgow (pages 17, 24, 27, 34, 36, 79, 87 bottom right, 119, 120); Angus Lamb (pages 23 and 75); Trustees of the National Museum of Scotland (pages 11, 19, 20, 50 bottom, 80, 88, 91); Trustees of the National Galleries of Scotland (page 103 bottom); Ordnance Survey (maps on end pages); the Royal Commission on the Ancient and Historical Monuments of Scotland (pages 12, 30, 33, 38, 50 top, 58, 100, 116); Römische-Germanisches Zentralmuseum, Mainz (page 69); the Society of Antiquaries of London (page 96); and the author (pages 53 and 54 bottom, 73, 87 top and left).

MEASUREMENTS

One Roman mile (*mille passuum*, that is 1,000 paces, one pace being 2 steps of 5 Roman feet) = 1,618 yards = 1,479m
One Roman foot = 11.64 imperial inches = 296 mm

EDGE

IPU 12 + . 11

WES

Author

Breeze, David

AL

EDGE OF EMPIRE

ROME'S SCOTTISH FRONTIER
THE ANTONINE WALL

C 02 0302441